Plum Jelly and Stained Glass & Other Prayers

Jo Carr & Imogene Sorley

Abingdon Press

Nashville　　　New York

Library of Congress Cataloging in Publication Data

CARR, JO.
    Plum jelly and stained glass & other prayers.
    1. Prayers. I. Sorley, Imogene, joint author.
    II. Title.
    BV245.C325   242'.8   72-14163

ISBN 0-687-31659-6

MANUFACTURED BY THE PARTHENON PRESS AT
NASHVILLE, TENNESSEE, UNITED STATES OF AMERICA

To that circle of friends
whose fellowship
strengthens and sustains us
and enriches our days

Lord,
The words were on a poster—
and I can't get them out of my mind:

YOU CAN FLY...
BUT THAT COCOON
HAS GOT TO GO.

And I don't think it was talking about butterflies.

But the risk—oh, the risk of leaving the swaddling
warmth of a cocoon. *My* cocoon. *My* status quo.
My . . . deadening security.
To leave the known,
no matter how confining it may be—for an *un-
known,* a totally new life-style—
oh, the risk!

Lord, my cocoon chafes, sometimes. But I *know*
its restrictions. And it's scary to consider the
awful implications of flight. I'm leery of heights.
(Even your heights.)
But, Lord, I could *see* so much wider, clearer
from heights.
And there's an exhilaration about flight that
I have always longed for.
I want to fly . . .
if I could just have the cocoon to come back to.
Butterflies can't.
I can't.
Probably butterflies don't even want to—
once they've tasted flight.

7

It's the risk that makes me hesitate.
The knowing I can't come back to the warm, unde-
   manding status quo.

Lord . . . about butterflies . . .
   the cocoon has only two choices—
      risk
      or die.
What about me?
If I refuse to risk,
   do I, too, die inside, still wrapped in the swaddling
   web?

                                          Lord?

Dear Lord,

I thought that maybe if I just ignored it, it would
go away. It didn't. It multiplied and magnified
instead.

I *hate* problems!
   We ought to be able to *cope* with them!
   This is the age of enlightened technology.
   People with our intelligence and experience and
      skill really *ought* to be able to *cope* with what-
      ever problem rears its ugly head.
It's so unsettling when we can't.

That's why I tried to ignore it.
Facing a problem is making myself vulnerable.
   Because maybe I can't cope.
      Then what?
So, I shove it back.
Put it off.
Cover it up.
Call it by another name.
Walk away from it.
Try—oh, try—to pretend it isn't there.
   Knowing all the time that it is.
   Knowing all the time that pretenses aren't valid.

So I come asking forgiveness for cowardice.
This is *my* problem, Lord! I shall pick it up.
Now.
I'm going to do all that I can do to solve it . . .
   all that I can do,

9

and then I'm going to put it down, and move on to
something else.

Problems are a gift.

The alternative life-style is puppetry.

Problems are a gift, and this one is mine.

Amen.

Oh, Lord, incomprehensible,
  Whom I alternately seek and ignore,
  forgive my inconstancy.
Sometimes I clamor so childishly at heaven's gates,
  demanding grace.
I want to be lifted right up out of my crummy everydayness into the transcendent joy of oneness with
  thee. Isn't that my *right?* Isn't that what it's all
  about?
Mostly, though, it doesn't come off, somehow. I
  don't find the exhilarating moment of glory, so . . .
  so I set the whole thing aside—putting it off
  until someday when I'll have time to clamor again
  at heaven's gates. Because right now I've got such
  a heap of crummy everydayness to attend to.

Oh, God, I don't want this kind of wishy-washy life.
This is not the kind of relationship I want with you
at all. And surely it cannot be the kind of relationship you want with me.

You are there, whether or not I clamor. You are
here.
  And my much-ado merely serves to focus my
mind on me. You are with me. Forgive my inconstancy. In thee do I trust.

Amen.

Dear Lord,

    it's easier to pray when everything's going my way, and I can yodel my thanksgiving for the gift of life.

But today just isn't that sort of day.
At the moment, my "gift" of life seems to have a price tag still attached.
My response is not one of thanksgiving.

I had everything arranged so well—
    and it isn't working out that way.
The orderly life that I had all planned for those I love is disordered—
        And steadfastly refuses to be put back into my structured "five-year plan."
    And I am undone.

Petty perfectionist that I am!
What Divine Sanction makes my five-year plan valid?
I'm not called to be their Manager.
    For these over whom I agonize have minds and lives and plans of their own.
It is my role not to manipulate them . . .
    but to accept them,
    and support them,
    and perhaps, on occasion, to enable them.

Hmm. I really don't *want* everything to go *my* way.
I shall put aside the role of manager—with deep relief.

It was a weighty and ill-fitting burden.

Now, then . . .
   now,
   I can say my thanksgiving for the gift of life.

Amen, amen.

God,

I need to let go of the past.

I've been carrying it like an albatross around my neck—and I can't get on with living because of a dead bird.

Not that there is anything wrong with the past—or with remembering the past.

But, ah, Lord . . .

She nurses an old grief, keeping it alive with ritual reminders, consciously renewing it until she has no desire to go on with the rest of living.

He dwells on a past failure, bound to it, and thus bound to repeat it, endlessly, in so many self-deprecating ways.

She glories in an old success, living only for a dusty laurel. Laurels can be albatrosses, too.

And I? Ah, Lord . . .

I, too, stand condemned.

I need to let go of my past, too.

My failure is a recent one.

My grief is new.

But let me remember, somehow, to keep both in perspective.

The past has brought me to this moment.

I am what I am because of the past.

But I am also called to go beyond the past— enabled by what it has taught me— to move into a new freedom.

Amen!

Lord,

How picayune of me—to have worried at such length over the color of paint for the hall closet!

How tedious of me—to have spent forty-five minutes debating over Texas hash versus Irish stew for supper.

How trivial—to have wasted choice moments deciding whether or not to go ahead and fill the ice tray.

Am I losing my marbles, Lord? Do I need a fidget stone?

What an incapacitating thing, to become incapable of making decisions at all!

Like J. Alfred Prufrock . . . "shall I part my hair behind? Do I dare to eat a peach?" [1] He mourned at the end because he had measured out his life with coffee spoons.

Is that what I'm doing? Have I become so . . . so jelly-fishy . . . that I'm living by morsels instead of full measure?

God, forbid!

You gave me a mind so I *could* make decisions. It is, after all, of no cosmic significance whether the closet is melon or mauve—

whether the supper is stew or hash.

I can make an arbitrary decision, knowing *it's really all right* either way—

and then have time enough, and mind enough,

to get on with weightier matters.

Vacillation behind me, I press on . . .

Amen.

[1] T. S. Eliot, "The Love Song of J. Alfred Prufrock."

Oh, Lord,
I keep remembering something your disquieting Son
said, in passing, one day by Galilee,
"Other sheep have I, which are not of this fold."

Other sheep—who do not bleat as I do? Ah hah!
This saying never seemed difficult to me, until this
year. I always thought he meant those sheep who
spoke languages other than my own. Same kind of
sheep like me, only they bleated with different ac-
cents.

Now I'm not so sure. What if the differences were
not *languages* but life-styles? What then?
Other sheep—observing other rituals.
Mouthing other prayers.
Worshiping thee in other ways I do not
understand.
Even those who speak in tongues unnerve me.
And these are thy sheep.
And thou art the shepherd.

Lord, it is a hard saying.
I find it easier to feel fellowship with those of other
faiths than with these of my own who do not feel as
I feel, or think as I think.
Why this blind spot? this *conceit?* that I should
think *my* way is best. How dull it would be if
all of us were alike. How unfair if we all had to
fit into a single pattern.

How great to have this freedom to *be* thy sheep,
each of us in his own creative way, relishing the
relationship with thee, and unhampered by the rigid-
ity of someone else's mold.

Amen.

I keep thinking about that "other sheep" bit, Lord.
I'm not real sure what Jesus meant, but I recall that
    he spent much of his time with the outcasts and
    oddballs. (Maybe they were more interesting to be
    with than some of us saintly types.)
My own hang-up has been, you know, with the
    counter-culture, with youth's defiance of *my* sacred
    cows.

> Long hair bugged me for awhile. Commune liv-
> ing threw me into a tizzy for some time.

But, Lord, the word from the cross is that we are all
of such value that the Son of Man was willing to
give his life that we might understand love.

> We are *all* loved. We are all accepted.

>> Even me?—even when my sanctimoniousness
>> gets in the way of loving?
>> Even when I set myself up as judge?

>>> Even me.
>>> Oh, Lord God—forgive.

>>>> Amen.

Lord,

it was one of those newfangled license plates that spell a word. The car was new, too . . . a small and rather sportish model, with a little old man at the wheel, and a little old lady beside him.

And the word on the license plate was GUSTO.

Oh, yes, Lord! *That's* the kind of little old lady I want to be! Facing life with gusto.

Surely that's the way you meant life to be lived. I recall something that was said about *abundant* living.

Lavish, cup-running-over.

It really doesn't have anything to do with sports cars, I know. But it has to do with enthusiasm (there's that word again—*entheos*—caught up in God). It has to do with awareness—eyes-open-to-life-ness—with getting outside myself.

Let me not grow little, growing old.

Let me not become all tied up in my own small package of aches and arthritis,

But let me be full of gusto—

full of enthusiasm?

full, Lord, of the sure knowledge that this is thy world—and that it is the best possible kind of world.

Little old lady?

Right, Lord—

but let me not wait for more birthdays to begin!

Lord, God,
I saw it happen—
Two people, sustained by the strength of their faith
   in thee, standing in the face of tragedy, standing in
   the midst of their agony—without bitterness.
It was not a faith dredged up for the occasion—it
was a *habit* of faith, an inner equilibrium, like a
gyroscope, that made it possible for them to meet
crisis. It was a faith established a long time ago,
matured and tested and sure. And the surety of it was
the knowledge of thy love.

> There was something exalted—exultant—about
> their strength. There was dignity even in the
> depth of their sorrow—and an affirmation in
> their grief.

Affirmation?
   That thou art God.
   That thou art Love.
   That life goes on
   And that, somehow, new strength, and new
      good, can come forth from the valley of the
      shadow.

Ah, Lord,
   thou art with us.

                                        Amen.

Lord,

He said it in the pastoral prayer—and it stood out suddenly for me . . . "I must not clamor for that portion of grace it would please me to receive, but must accept with grateful wonder that which falls to me."

I WANT MORE, LORD!

I want voices, visions, and blessed assurance.
    And all I've got is the nagging knowledge that thou
        art Mystery, and that the search is endless.
    Others see more than I do—
    and understand with greater certainty.
    It would have pleased *me,* too, to have received
    such a portion of grace.
    But that is not the portion that has fallen to me.
        It is mine to search and not quite find, to
            glimpse rather than to gaze upon—
                to be certain only of the uncertainty of
                that which I must pursue.
Lord, let me not clamor. Grant me the humility to accept my role.

I thank thee for the grace that has fallen to me.
I stand in awe before my glimpses of thy glory.
        Thine *is* the kingdom, and the power. Thine
        is the glory.
            And mine is the search.
                Praise God, from whom all
                blessings flow. Amen, amen.

Ah, Lord—
   The handed-down Word-by-mouth finally-written
   Message opens with the clear affirmation:
      In the beginning, God.
And now, God.
Always and always, God.

Then man.
Then me.
Now me. This strikes me with almost as much
   impact . . .
   I am.

Where I go, I know not.
But it is *I* who go . . .
   this entity which is me.
   this unique and unrepeatable combination of
      genes, with a potential all my own.
Quo vadis?
¿Quien sabe?
   But I go.
There is work in the world to be done—work that I
alone may be able to do—in that moment and in
that place where I am. I am needed, by the Lord
God Almighty! It's a spine-tingling clarion call, and
I go. . . . My everlasting life has already begun.

                                          Amen.

Dear Lord,
I come contritely.

My *neighbor* is retarded, and I never realized it before.

> That *he* was my neighbor, I mean. I knew that Edna, down the block, had a grown brother who was retarded. Edna's my neighbor, Lord.
> > *But so is David.* And for four years I've pretended he wasn't there. I don't know *anything* about retarded people—especially adults—so I've looked past him, or sometimes condescended to wave. Mostly, I've just pretended that he wasn't there.

I have trouble remembering that he is a person—and that what you expect of him is precisely the same that you expect of me—to be the very best person he can be with the gifts that are his.

Hmm . . . he is a person.

> *Persons* hunger for human contact. I wonder how many *other* people pretend David isn't there? Is this the world he knows—just himself, and familiar Edna, and a host of blank, unseeing faces?
> > *Persons* hunger for self-esteem—the sort that comes from making a worthy contribution. Lord, I wonder—what *are* the worthy contributions David could make? *Is* he good with plants? *Would* he respond to the orderly workings of an engine? I don't even know him well enough to guess. But if I went over there for coffee—and *met* my neighbor David

22

—I might learn enough to see some way of
enabling him.
I might even discover a friend, as well as a neighbor.
Father, forgive my long delay.

I go.

Lord, I haven't accomplished a thing all day.
    And it's been great!

This morning I stood out in the yard.
    Just stood,
      and looked,
      and smelled,
      and listened.
    A mockingbird sang matins for me.
    Roses and peach trees scented my reverie.
    And I saw jewels . . . rubies and emeralds and
      gorgeous things hanging on the fence,
      left over from last night's rain.

I squandered half the afternoon with a book,
    the other half with a friend.

And then, we went on a picnic.
    The kids chortled and cavorted.
    I hadn't squished mud through my toes for years!

It's been a delightful, renewing, refreshing day,
Lord—
    and I give thanks for it.

                        Amen.

God,

I watch my fledgling children perched on the edge
of our nest, ready and eager and anxious for
flight into adulthood—

and I tremble, even as I thrill at the wonder of
it all.

Lord, have they learned, somewhere, somehow, those
things that will hold them steady amidst the dif-
ficulties and the delights that will be a part of
their lives?

Have we protected them too much—or not enough?

Have we let them be *too little* buffeted by the real
world—bound them in swaddling clothes and
apron strings?

Or have we pushed *too* hard, permitting them
to be *too much* hurt?

Ah, Lord, what is their vision, as they hover on the
nest's edge? Do they sense thy divine scheme of
things—and the part they can play in it?

I pray this day for them, that they may slip the
bonds of child-life, and know the joy of flight!

Amen.

Lord,
   why is everything that's a virtue also a vice?
It makes the vices harder to recognize.
   Honesty . . . becomes callousness.
   Determination deteriorates to muleheadedness.
   Concern, overdone, smothers.
   Diligence, loyalty, self-confidence—even piety?—
      can be carried to sinful excess.

So where's the line of demarcation?
Honesty *is really* a good thing. How do I manage to
make it a vice? That's what happens when I become
more concerned with the *virtue* than with the *people*. Self-focus again. Self-consciousness. Noble, pious
me, Lord. I'M HONEST!

   I use it as a club to keep everybody else at a
distance, by keeping myself untainted and superior.

   Or I use it as a ticket—guaranteed to get me
into heaven, because *you* know I never lie!—self-
salvation?

   Some virtue!

Oh Lord! what a web of self-deceit we weave around
   ourselves with these threads of virtue—and how
   far we stray from thee.
We?
I, Lord.

   By trying to *save* myself I damn myself. When
. . . oh, when . . . will I get the *self* out of the
center of my thinking?

                                        When?

Lord,

my life is such a mess that I've got to pick up before I can carry on.

Like my desk gets. Clutter and responsibilities, piled up indiscriminately, to such awesome heights that I can't find a thing. Can't *do* a thing until I stop and sort it out.

Ah, so.

It's easier to do with my desk than it is with my life. The things on the desk are more immediate, I guess—or more graphic. I can perceive more readily the need for them—or the uselessness of them.

But responsibilities of *living* get buried under clutter, too.

When I let the search for the precise shade of shoes to match a dress become a Search—

when I let a hairdresser's appointment become a tyranny—

when I leave a dearly beloved friend unvisited because I haven't time—

am I forgetting what the priorities are?

The desk is easier to sort when I decide what the goal is, and get on with it.

The priorities of living are easier to sort when I decide where I'm going to put my life.

You ask hard things, Lord.

But the hard things you ask make all the little other things so much easier. The lucidity of that *one* decision clarifies the rest.

I've got to sort things out now, so I can carry on.

Amen.

About this matter of accomplishing things—

My endless lists are useful. They keep me on my toes.
But sometimes they keep me pecking away at the
trivia and I miss out on the truly significant. I
huffle around cleaning out a drawer when I could
be changing history!

> Like the Pussy Cat, Pussy Cat,
> who went—oh, chance of a lifetime—
> to visit the *queen!*
> . . . and blew it, chasing a mouse.

Ah, Lord!
The lists *do* help. But only if they *free* me to do
worthier things. Lists are no help if they *bind* me to
their predicated practicality.

> I can *change* my list! Abbreviate it. Even toss
> it out, if it becomes holy writ to me.

Guide thou the planning of my days.
And let me not blow *my* chance of a lifetime pur-
suing something less than thy will.

Amen.

Lord,
the music of the spheres rings discordant in my ears
tonight.

    Are mosquitoes and fire ants and poison oak really
    necessary in the divine Scheme of Things?

"These things are sent to try us," my pious neighbor
says.

    You wouldn't. Would you? That seems unseemly
    of God Almighty.

And yet—this *is* your world. And this is the way
    you've created it—

        full of all sorts of possibilities . . .

            wild iris—and poison oak,
            mosquitoes, yes—but cardinals and morning
                glories, too.

The irksome extras sent to *try* us, Lord?

    Are they just the natural result of the built-in
    freedom that makes possibilities possible?

        Human possibilities, too. No robot could have
        written the *Messiah*. And prayers prattled
        by a push-button doll wouldn't have meant
        much, even to the Creator.

I'd rather be free, swatting mosquitoes, than even
the noblest of push-button dolls. Fire ants and poison
oak are merely flies in the ointment. They needn't
throw me—for they are, after all, such *little* things.

    And the world—this thy wondrous world—
    is full of all sorts of possibilities.

                         Amen.

Lord,

There is a joy that I have known that is five parts jubilance and one part ignorance. It's that soft-headed, naïve sort of joy that Pippa sings of:

> The year's at the spring
> And day's at the morn;
> Morning's at seven;
> The hillside's dew-pearled;
> The snail's on the thorn.
> The lark's on the wing;
> God's in his heaven—
> All's right with the world! [1]

But all's not right with *my* world. You know that my problems are not the trifling sort that tomorrow dispels. You know, Lord, that my sorrows are not easily dismissed.

> But, oh, I thank you, Father-God, for that other, deeper joy—
>> that comes *in spite of*—nay, *because of,* the problems. The burdens would be too much, without the joy. The joy would be empty out of context.

Joy-in-full-awareness.

Joy *anyway*.

> My cup runneth over—
> with joy and thanksgiving.

---

[1] Robert Browning, "Pippa Passes."

Lord,
    after looking at me—
what do my children think of growing old?
    Do they see aging as a sort of slow torture that
fate has in store?
        I grump.
        I moan about corns and bursitis and getting
            poofed-out.
        I nag.
        And lecture.
        And advise . . . oh, how I do advise! (Does it
            say anywhere that wisdom is like compound
            interest? What makes me think I'm smarter
            just because I'm older?)

    I *like* getting older, Lord! Forgive me—and help
them forgive me—when I give the wrong impression.
Help me to remember to be *at least* as articulate
about the new possibilities that are open to me *because* of my age.

    Yesterday was great. *But today is more so*. And I
can't wait for tomorrow! This is no time for past-dwellers. This is the day that thou hast made.
    I *do* rejoice in it—
        I just forget to say so.

                                Amen.

Dear Lord and Father of mankind,
  forgive our feverish ways!
Feverish—frantic.

    Hurry and get the committee meeting rolling or it
  won't be over in time for the scheduled next one.
      Much to do. Much ado.
    And often very little done.
    Except for headaches and ulcers and overfatigue.
Forgive my feverish ways.
Is this *really* the way the work of the kingdom gets
done?
Oh, Lord, why do I try to measure the quality of life
by the number of meetings I go to every week? The
number of boards and commissions and committees
I'm on?

    I have a responsibility to assist on worthy com-
  munity projects. I have a responsibility to stand
  in the yard and be blessed by apple blossoms,
  too. And I have responsibilities to family and to
  self.

        All of which are part of my responsibility
  to thee. The dither comes in letting it get
  out of perspective—in getting so tied up
  in "good works" that I can't function.
Gracious Lord, forgive my feverish ways.

                         Amen.

Dear Lord and Father of mankind,
   forgive our foolish ways.

I sing it, idly, wishing that thy will might indeed be done, thy kingdom come. My notions as to how this shall come to pass, however, are vague and fuzzy, and quite disoriented.

Forgive my foolish ways. Idle thoughts do not contribute to kingdom-building. My unfocused wishful thinking has not yet *solved any*thing. Even my pious attempts at good works are ineffective. I've been taking a Christmas basket to "The Needy" every December 24th for ten years—and they are still hungry. Even if I organized all my friends to take Christmas baskets, the gesture would still be only a bandaid on a malignant wound.

   Lord, forgive my foolish ways. I know that what it takes to solve problems is hard, sweaty work—lucidity—the focused mind.

   There is nothing romantic about real evaluation or the clearheaded setting of long-term goals. There is nothing emotional about dividing the goals into chunks—how much has to be done by the ninth year if we're going to achieve our objective by the tenth. What portion must be done now?

   This sort of work earns no brownie points. It probably won't even get written up in my obituary.

   But it solves problems. It helps bring in the kingdom. And there is thrill in being part of it that "foolish ways" can't touch!

   Amen. Amen.

Lord,
my family stands in need of—
of a strength that is not in my power to give.
Even if I had it I could not give it.

> I can feed them,
> I can mend their jeans.

>> But I cannot give them the one thing they
>> need most—that is a faith—a strength—to
>> live by.
>> Strong physique isn't enough to support the
>> spirit when life falls in,

>>> and the faith that *is* enough is not only
>>> un-purchasable but un-givable.

I can lead them in what I feel to be right directions,
Lord—and I can live before them the best way that
I know how.

> *That's all that I can do*—and it isn't enough.

Lord, God—give them strength.
Pursue them. Grant them no peace until they find
that peace is in thee.

> Lure them into finding the faith that will help
> them stand steady in the world.

Amen.

Father,

I've always sort of ached for the lonely—in general.

But this was *my child!* His long-distance phone
call last night . . .

"What are you doing, Jim?"

"Walking around town watching all the other
lonely people."

It stood out sharp for me, because it was Jim.
Lonely.

Like the stranger in the apartment house down *my*
street is lonely,

like the student who sits alone at church,

like the widow whose children are grown and
gone—so very gone,

like the tied-up mother of toddlers who is lonely
in the midst of her houseful of kids.

Oh, Lord, there are so *many* lonely ones.

And loneliness is cold.

To protect my own privacy, I try not to notice—
"lest I intrude." They, anxious not to *appear* lonely,
hide behind facades of cheerfulness on purpose. And
I, anxious *not* to notice, nod and smile and go my
way. The almost-contact is flubbed because neither of
us dared reach out.

And the utter loneliness goes on, just becom-
ing a little more miserable.

It's not right in a world so full of people that anyone
is lonely. I can't do much about Jim, half a con-
tinent away—but I can do something about these
within my reach whose loneliness is here.

I can draw the circle that takes them in.

Today?

Amen. Today!

Ah, Lord—

This is my stained-glass window today!

Seventeen jars of plum jelly—lined up on the kitchen sill, where sunlight can play through them and brighten my world.

This is the essence of summer, caught in a jar.

Summer, savored.

Ah, so.

Then there is more than jelly to be put up.

I need to preserve some of the deliberately under-taken *fun* of these not-so-scheduled summer days. I shall bottle some, to serve again like cherry wine some midwinter's evening when the color of joy has been almost forgotten.

I shall capture the flavor of a whole long lazy August day, to remember in December.

I shall preserve in some chamber of my mind the color of lilac, the lilting clarity of larksong—and the warmth of summer sun upon my back.

Winter shall have delights of its own, I know. But I shall enjoy them all the more because of the saved and savored color of summer on my shelf.

Thank you, Lord.

Ah, Lord!
There is lemon-colored paint in my hair—and on
my knees and up my arms—

>and the smell of fresh paint permeates the
>whole house. The bathroom is like new! The old
>tile looks fresh and clean and bright. Even the
>corners are sparkling.

What is it about fresh paint that lifts the spirit and
makes *me* feel clean—and bright—

>like a new beginning,
>like permission to start afresh.
>Housekeeping is so much easier—and so much
>more fun—after the renewal.

Ah, so. Minds, too. When I really clean out the
corners of my life, setting some worthy goals and
making some major decisions—it's like a renewal.
Like the smell of fresh paint.

>It's so much less complicated to live in such
>a setting.

Oh, Lord God—help me be aware of my *need* for
rejuvenation.
It's easier to *see* the need when the bathroom tiles
fall into the tub. Worn-out ideas and rusting attitudes
are less obvious.

>*Keep* me aware. Prod me, Lord, that I may
>keep after the corners.

>And renew my spirit.

>>Amen.

Perhaps, Lord, there should have been an eleventh commandment—for me:

> "Thou shalt not bludgeon thy family with the club of thine own weariness."

I come home from work so tired that all I can think of is heaving a great sigh and getting this weight off my feet.

> And if one of my children is waiting for me, with a joy to share—or a burden of weariness of her own—she will not share it if she sees me brandish my club.

Ah—today, Lord, let me come in from work and sigh a *gentle* sigh, and make a glass of tea for her, too, clinking the ice in it cheerily as I stir—sharing a giggle with her over the sheer luxury of taking off my shoes and wiggling my toes, as we sit down to relax pleasantly together.

> Moaning about how tired I am usually serves to make me more so.

> But resting creatively gives a second wind.

Today, Lord, let me not beat off my family with the club of my *self*-conscious weariness.

Amen.

Lord, God Almighty,
   Creator of artichokes and cicadas' wings.
   Designer of infinity—
        and designer of me, too—
   hear, oh, hear my prayer.

Hear my prayer for goodness. I have too often been
content with goody-goodyness, which is not the same.
   There is a *good*-ness, a genuineness about artichokes and cicadas, about *all* of nature. Everything seems to fill its own niche, do its own
   thing, without pretense. I pray for such an
   honesty, a self-acceptance.

Hear my prayer for unity. You must have pleasured
in the small things of your creation.
   They have such crisp and clean detail. There is
   no fuzziness of line about leaf veins—no
   meandering absence of pattern about spider
   webs. Let there be orderliness and clean de-
   sign in me as well. Let there be a clear centered-
   in-thee-ness to my life-style.

        Lord of the universe, hear my prayer.

Dear Lord,

Paul was a long time ago.

So were those church-folk in Corinth.

And the words are so old and familiar that I catch myself not hearing them anymore. Maybe I need to put them in my own vernacular.

I may use polished rhetoric, and speak inspiringly, but if I do so without really caring about people, my eloquence is wasted.

I might have a mind like Einstein's, and a gift of clairvoyance, and I might have been a churchgoer all my life—but if I don't care about people, I'm nothing.

I could pack Christmas baskets to feed the poor every year—I could even give away everything I own—but if I did it without being sensitive to the needs behind the hunger, it wouldn't be enough. *Care*-less sacrifice would bring no lasting benefit to them or to me.

Those who really care put up with a lot. They love the unlovely. They understand. They accept. Theirs is a sort of caring that puts self in third place. Theirs is the sort of caring that neither boasts nor feels that it has the right to boast.

Those who care are innately courteous. Because they care, they are able to step out beyond the four cozy walls of their own group. They have a supportive trust in people. And they don't get miffed over little things.

Those who care about others take no pleasure in *using,* or *abusing,* them, and find no satisfaction in participating in gossip about them.

There is no wearing down of their spirit. They have an inner certainty that life is good, and from this stance they embrace it all—death as well as birth, sorrow as well as joy.

Caring is constant. But those who foretell the future sometimes goof. Those who speak in tongues may on occasion be misinterpreted. Those who study and analyze may lose their notes. Those who genuinely care, though, can be counted on.

We don't know all the answers. It may be that we don't even know all the questions. That's all right!

For ultimately the kingdom will be made perfect, and our human imperfections are already accepted as part of it.

Childishness is fine, for kids. But I'm not a kid anymore. It's time I grew up and became one of the concerned.

I catch only a glimpse, know only a smattering, of what the kingdom would be if everyone really cared.

> (Thy kingdom come, Lord.
> Thy will be done.)

Three virtues last—conviction, optimism, and concern.

> But the greatest of these is concern.

Dear Lord—
    Uh . . .
    guide my naysaying!

I have fits of agreeing to anything—
    yes, I'll be on both those committees,
    sure, I'll be the room mother,
    yes, I'll lead the program,
    yes, I'll join the study group.
And then I get overscheduled—and irked with "them" for asking me, and annoyed with myself for having agreed—and I don't do a very creative or contributive job of anything.
        So I start saying "no."
        Indiscriminately.

And turn down real opportunities to be of use to thee—turn down once-in-my-lifetime chances to be a part of something worthy—to throw the puny ounces of my weight where it would count. And then I *do* feel guilty.
        Lord, guide my naysaying.
Give me the wisdom, and the audacity, to say the right thing.
Partly it's a matter of thinking through the priorities.
Once I do that, I have a basis for making the smaller decisions.
Don't let me say yea or nay automatically—indiscriminately.
        Guide thou my naysaying.

                                        Amen.

Lord,

sometimes thy blessings rain down upon me in almost incomprehensible abundance. It seems that the windows of heaven are opened up and I exult and rejoice in the downpour.

But I think I could not bear it, Lord, if every day were like that. My soul would become surfeited—and my exultation a weariness.

Small rains, too, make gardens grow.

I'm deeply grateful for the ordinary everydays, when thy blessings come down upon me gently, as summer showers.

> There is a calm to such blessings,
>> a time to bask in them.

> The *quiet* awareness of your presence brings a *sustaining* strength—a strength that enables us to hold steady, through both the great moments and the dark nights of the soul.

There's a security and a comfort in the everyday showers of gentle blessings.

> Thank you, Lord God.

Lord, I know a push-button doll. She is pre-programmed to do and say all the right things. There is a studied poise about her, an urbane polish.

And I envy her ability to carry life off so smoothly.

But there's something . . . plastic . . . about her life-style. I'm never really *warmed* in her presence. I'm *impressed,* but not strengthened. Somehow her humanness is missing. She's too predictably correct.

Ah, Lord, I have my push-button reactions, too—when I say the pre-programmed cliché instead of allowing myself to become involved with a *human* response.

I mouth the traditional platitudes—react in the way that I suppose that I'm supposed to react.

And there is no *humanness* in it. No *me* in it—just push-button response. It won't answer human need, and I know it.

Now that I think of it, Lord—there's not much difference between me and my push-button friend—just that she's so much more elegant. And there is no virtue in my being graceless.

What both of us need is to jam our computers. I'm *not* a computer! I am a human being, made in thy image, made to be me. I'm not pre-programmed with right answers, but created to respond to others who are also unique.

Lord, help me to respond.

Lord, there's something despicable about *using* people.

  I don't mean like the business tycoon who climbs to his millions over the broken backs of others. That's too obvious.

I mean the way I do—

  anytime I participate in "putting down" another living soul,

  anytime I laugh *at,* not *with* another,

  when I try to arrange my children's lives so they will be "nice" exhibits of my own fine qualities as a mother,

  when I nag my husband into a promotion I know he doesn't want, so that I can enjoy the benefits.

Using people—using friendships—to satisfy my own ego. I forget, sometimes, about human dignity—about my responsibility to support the basic worth of people.

  And in the forgetting, I do despicable things.

  Lord, let me never belittle the worth of another, nor boost my own ego, ever, at the cost of human dignity.

Amen.

Father,

I've been crying over my child's "spilt milk,"
 which is useless.

  He's reached the age where the decisions are his
   own.

  His is the milk, and his is the mess—
   and his is the right and the responsibility to
   clean it up.

My blubbering will only serve to confuse the issue.

He is always my son, Lord—but his decisions are
 no longer my responsibility. It is essential—for his
 sake—that I let him go. I believe in him—believe
 in his ability to come through this crisis and
 others—believe in his ability to stand alone. Why
 do I deny that belief with motherly blubbering?

Besides, I have promises of my own to keep, and
 things to do and miles to go before I sleep.

Watch over my son, Lord.

Amen. Amen.

Father God,
In these small early hours when the rest of my family still sleeps, I listen for the sounds of the waking world. I'm tuned in for the song of the cardinal, but all I hear is two motorcycles and a delivery truck.

"This is my Father's world," the hymn affirms. "All nature sings!"

Hmmm. There was rustling grass and the song of the cardinal after what Genesis refers to as the fifth day of creation. And you saw that it was good. And you saw that it was not enough. And so you made man—free, bungling man—and saw that he was good, too.

This is thy world! Motorcycles and delivery trucks are a part of it!

Man is a part of it, and the sound of a truck should be as valid a call to worship as the lyric melody of a bird.

Ah, Lord, what makes me think I can experience thy presence only in a pastoral setting? Only at a mountain retreat? Or a calm corner in the city park?

You are *here*—the *present* Presence— in the marketplace and on the city bus.

Let me remember.

Lord,
> the hardest part of a real problem is being able to quit worrying about it after I've done everything I can to resolve it.

When I've done all I can, I should leave it with thee.
> Only I don't.
> I still carry it like a millstone around my neck.

I ought to be able to trust thee enough to let it go.
I *say* I do . . . I *think* I do . . .
> but I keep on carrying the millstone. I keep on worrying it over in my mind, keep turning it over and over with a paralyzing preoccupation—
>> until I am unable to get on with *anything* else.

Lord, how *can* I go on, encumbered as I am?

I know from past experience that peace comes only when I am finally unable to go any farther under my own steam. It is only then, in a sort of *desperation,* that I am forced to trust in thee *enough* to let it go.

Why is it that I can't remember this? Why do I have to go to the point of desperation *every time?*

I do not pray, Lord, for release from burdens that I can bear. Give me strength *to do all I can,* wisdom to see any possible answers to my dilemma—
> and then, when I have done what *I* can do, Lord,
>> take my burden.

Sometimes I don't even *read* what's on the back of the church bulletin.

But this one, Lord—this one confronted me:

> "People who go flying around the moon don't think, act, or live like people who walked all day behind two mules and a plow."

The times they are a-changing, and I—we—are caught up in it. These "new days" are neither better nor worse than the "old days."

> The point is that you have placed *me* in the new day. And my commission is to accept it,
>
> embrace it, and minister to it in your name.

Lord, I keep trying to think and live as though I were walking behind that plow—

> slow and easy,
>
> provincial,
>
> tradition-bound.

I'm not sure I know how to think new ways, how to create new and out-reaching traditions through which to minister in your name.

But *ministering* is what it's all about.

> And the day is new.
>
> And good.
>
> And yours.
>
> And I am yours.

Amen.

Dear Lord,
>   there are times when what I *really* need is the
>   courage to go first!
>>   . . . like skiing out across virgin snow in a new
>>   venture, not following someone else's tracks,
>>   not knowing where the pitfalls are
>>   . . . but daring to risk the pitfalls in order to do
>>   the necessary deed.
But I'm reluctant.
Scared, Lord.
Too insecure to go first.
>   There are times—*when the goal is worth it*—
>   that I need to throw caution to the wind and push
>   out first. When the goal is worth it.
You have not called me to be foolhardy for nothing.
>   But you may have called me to risk the security of
>   my quiet life in order to be one of those foolhardy-
>   for-something souls who change history.
And, oh, the exhilarating joy there must be in skiing
across virgin snow! I crave this kind of exhilaration—
even as I stand shaking in my shoes.
>>   The goal, the risk—the exultant joys—
>>   could be mine, Lord?

>>>>   Let it be.

Lord,
    could we celebrate . . .
    uh . . . Tuesday?

This is no official holiday—
no act of Congress sets it aside as special—
it isn't even labeled on the calendar.
It isn't the end of anything—
    like Thank God, It's Friday—
or the beginning of anything—
    like Oh, Lord, It's Monday Again.
It's just Tuesday. But there has been something
jubilant about it from the moment of waking. And
it needs celebrating.

*   *   *   *   *

For this most wondrous day,
We thank you, God—
for the beauty of earth spread out before us—
for the mystery of faith written within us—
for the challenge of life you place around us.
We thank you, God, for *this* most wondrous day.

Amen!

"The earth is the Lord's, and the fulness thereof;
the world, and they that dwell therein.
For he hath founded it upon the seas
and established it upon the floods."

And we, Lord, have defiled it—
and endangered it—
out of selfishness and ignorance and unconcern.
Lord, I have not the right to clutter up the face of the
earth with non-returnable bottles.
Nor does my family have the right to produce its ton
of trash this year.
Nor does my church have the right to ignore its responsibility in calling us to account. The quality of
life on this thy earth is at stake—and we cannot
simply sit here mouthing platitudes. The quality of
life is what the church is all about.
It's a matter of stewardship, Lord. A matter of ac-
cepting my responsibility, and my church's responsibility for getting something done.

Don't let me get so glutted with all the *words* I hear
about pollution that I am no longer aware of an imperative for deeds, a *divine* imperative!
There's a *religious* implication here that the
man of faith cannot ignore.
The earth is *thine,* Lord. And I, and my church,
are responsible to thee for the way we take care
of it.

Amen.

Lord,
   some kid wrote it on the classroom blackboard—
      "I am neither for nor against apathy."
I laughed,
and then I shuddered, aware that some people really
   are apathetic.
And then I stood incriminated—
   remembering that I, who think I feel so strongly
   about *not* being lukewarm, *am*.

I pore over the appalling statistics on world popu-
lation. But I didn't volunteer to help when my
church agreed to co-sponsor the neighborhood
planned parenthood clinic.

I don't study enough to know enough to stand
up for much of anything. So I sit in the committee
meeting trying to look wise, and contribute
nothing. That's a form of apathy.

So is forgetting (not bothering?) to save tin cans
for the recycling project.

So is my unwillingness to voice disagreement
when it needs to be articulate. I disguise it as
respect for the opinions of others." But really, it's
apathy.

So is my *casual* awareness of slums, and jails, and
lonely neighbors.

Father, seventy *times* seven, forgive *my* apathy!

                                        Amen.

Lord,

I've noticed that the people who get there are generally the ones who know where they are going . . .

not like me, meandering aimlessly through my days . . .

but setting off intentionally along a plotted route. Hmm. They know where they are going.

I wouldn't consider starting out on a *vacation* without some preliminary decisions, but I can live whole years at a time without any goals beyond next week.

No wonder I get lost on little bypaths.

No wonder all kinds of superficial things claim my attention.

No wonder I never really arrive.

Goals again—and setting my mind to hard thinking about *how* I shall spend this only life that is mine to spend.

Lord, guide my goal-setting.

Amen.

Lord,
    there seems to be that counter-side to every coin—
    and though it's true enough that I'll never reach
    my goals without deciding where I'm going . . .
    don't let me miss all the little goodies along the
    way!
        They are the bonuses that make the trip so
        much more delightful.
Some days, I'm so *me*-getting-on-with-*my*-goals con-
scious that I am totally unaware of choice and unexpected friendships along the way—friendships that
might have enriched my journey, if I had been
open to them.
    I am oblivious to the opportunities for learning
    new things, for acquiring new skills and mind-
    opening insights—when I'm overly route-con-
    scious.
        And *little* goodies . . . the dew-studded
        symmetry of a spider web . . . the dearness
        of a small child . . . the unconscious grace
        of a cat . . . the bowl of a tulip . . . a
        dandelion fluff . . . Lord, let me not be too
        preoccupied to notice.
For once I have determined the direction my life
shall take, I need not keep my eyes riveted on the
next footstep. The goal-setting gives me freedom to
enjoy the treasures I may encounter.

        Thank you, Lord, for the
        goodies along my way.

Lord,

why is it that even with my own children I get tongue-tied—and can't say the things that are aching to be said?

All I can get said is "Good-bye," and "Have a good trip!" and "Take care."

And they are gone—perhaps without even knowing the love in which they are held—the pride I have in them—the faith. The memories of a thousand shared joys—aches—problems—crazy moments of fun—are there

. . . but all I can say is "Take care."

Maybe there aren't any words. But, dear Lord, let my message get through to them, somehow. Help them understand that some things are beyond saying. Some moments are more than tongue can tell—or heart can hold in silence. And the meaningless words I manage to say are fraught with love.

I guess they know, Lord,

. . . even as I know, through *their* tongue-tied good-bye and unsaid affection, the bond of love that continues to unite us. I'm grateful, Lord, that it doesn't have to depend on words.

Bless us with thy unspoken word— thy unspoken love.

Amen.

Thank you, God,
for little humdrum jobs like peeling apples and washing dishes.

> They give me a *chance* to communicate with my children.

There's something about having my hands busy that frees my mind—that permits my thinking to rise above the humdrum tasks. And there's something about being involved in a common task that unites us.

> And we talk . . .
>> "Remember the time when . . .?"
>> "What do you think about. . .?"
>> "I use to feel that way, too."
>> "Have you read . . . ?"
>> "The other day my teacher said . . ."
>> "I wonder . . ."

Our minds wander along together while our hands are busy with the task.

> Thank you, Father, for such humdrum tasks . . .
> and for these who do them with me.

Amen.

Dear God,

have I joined the cult of the clock worshipers?
Am I so concerned with having everything run on schedule that I don't even hear The Question, if it's asked at ten minutes to five?

> The Question—that someone's finally got up the nerve to ask—The Problem, that someone's finally become ready to face—the lonely agony that someone is only now able to share—
>
>> except that I am *unable,* because of the clock.

Ah, Lord—*is it so vital* that I leave on time? Every time?

Who is in command here—thee, or me, or the clock?

Am I rendered incompetent by an implacable mechanical device that tells me "Thou shalt"?

> I shall not!
>
> Lord, the imperatives are thine.
>
> The decisions are mine.
>
> The clock is merely a device.
>
> I shall not let *it* become my god.

Amen.

When I consider the Pleiades
and Betelgeuse and Orion—
and stars beyond stars whose names I do not know,
I am wonder-struck,
for thy creation is so far beyond my ability to com-
    prehend.

And I am still, as the night is still,
    for the stars are so far—
    and you, Lord, so inexplicably near.

I am humbled, Lord, for what am I that *you* are
    mindful of *me?*

And I am filled with quiet exultation that my life and
    times are in thy hands.

Oh, Lord, I celebrate this holy night.

                                    Amen.

Lord God,

   I am disturbed by the cry of those "skillful in
   lamentation."

They mourn over the passing of the earth, and weep
over the imminent death of man—and copious indeed
are the tears they shed.

         But by then they are so sated with grief that they
         are too weary to roll up their sleeves and set to
         work, to help right the wrongs that we have
         perpetrated upon ourselves.

We *are* in an ecological mess, Lord. *I* can see it—
more clearly every year. I'm sure the earth scientists
can see it more clearly than I. The haze on the far
horizon that used to herald the arrival of autumn,
now testifies to the presence of exhaust fumes. We
ourselves are an endangered species.

         But lamentations won't solve earth's problems.
         Prophecies of doom only engender a "why
         bother, then?" sort of apathy.

                  The earth is yours, Lord. And it's redeem-
                  able.

                  And *we* are yours, and we can redeem it.
                  You have given us mind and hands and
                  heart enough to tackle the mess we're in.

There is no time for lamentations. We have much to
do.

                                          Amen.

Dear Lord,
   I thank you that I do not *always* flub it.

   Once in awhile I *do* happen to be at the right
place, at the right time,
   sufficiently aware of another to say at least a few
      of the right words.
   And for this I give thanks.

   There have been so many occasions when someone
else has *been* for me what I needed—
   given me strength,
   or served as the beloved opponent—
      argued with me, counseled me—
   helped me bear, or face, my troubles—
   helped me celebrate my joys.

And now, *this* time, I have had the opportunity to
undergird someone else. And I didn't flub it.
   I am grateful, Lord. Grateful to those who have
helped me—grateful that this once I forgot myself
enough to priest to another.

                        Thank you, Lord.
                        Amen.

God,

I guess it never occurred to me that after years of struggle, it would continue to *be* a struggle—keeping my mind stayed on thee. I thought it would be automatic by now. I guess I thought I would be . . . uh . . . habitually sanctified.

But I see, Lord, that it doesn't work that way. For just as I begin to feel that I have made great progress in my spiritual quest, that I am really beginning to understand "things of the spirit," I come instead to some dark night of the soul . . . and I cannot reach thee. My prayers seem no more than random words written on paper airplanes and thrown at the sky. *I cannot reach thee, Lord.* The feelings of peace and blessed surety for which I long are not there. I cannot grasp the Psalmist's declaration that "thou art with me"—but cry instead with Elijah, "Oh, that I knew where I might find thee!"
So that's the way it is, Lord?—always a struggle? Always alternating between the brilliance of midday —and a groping in the dark?

The only surety I have is that there *will* be these dark nights of the soul—and that there *will* be, as there have been, the times of close and personal *experience* of thy presence. Ah so, Lord. This is thy way.

Help me remember, in my times of groping, that the way will be clear . . . for awhile. And in my times of blessed surety, that thou art Mystery, and that there will again be times when the way is dark.

Bless the Lord, oh my soul,
and all that is within me—
bless his holy name.

Thank you, God, for these continuing friendships
that are the legacy of shared grief.

The difficult times that we endured together
have revealed us to ourselves and to each other
—so that now there is no need for sham, or for
protective masks. Before these persons, I can
still stand, unveiled.

For awhile they knew me with all my humanness ex-
posed—and accepted me as I was. This mutual
acceptance has been part of the bond. Because
of it, we can talk at a greater depth—get to the
heart of a matter without the need for conversa-
tional preambles.

And I come away renewed. And steadied.

Things fall into a *different* perspective when I
am not obliged to wear my mask. So I come
away renewed.

I thank you, God, for this fellowship,
born of adversity,
that continues to uphold me.

Amen.

Lord, God,

I am possessed by legions of *things,* even as the Gadarene was possessed.

I speak of my *things* as possessions—
but it is I who am possessed.

I am fettered, bound to routine and structured days—by the tyranny of things.

> I ought to visit the sick, but I haven't finished dusting the knickknacks.

> I need to feed the hungry, but I've got to stay home and water the grass.

> The naked are waiting to be clothed, but I've got to take the stereo to the shop.

I have allowed my life to become so cluttered with possessions that I am rendered ineffective. I forget about people. I don't have time to be bothered with them.

> Gradually, insidiously, *things* have become the possessor, and I the possessed.

It is not that material possessions in themselves are bad. They can be tools, enabling me to do what I really *need* to do.

But my priorities are misplaced when I focus on the things themselves, and not on what they can enable me to do.

> Dear Lord, deliver me from the tyranny of things.

> Restore my perspective—*thy* perspective.

Amen.

Ah, Lord,
>how lucky am I!
>Blessed with the best of both worlds—
>>I have home and family—
>>*and* a satisfying job!

I remember now how I blubbered about having to go
to work.
>But on this first anniversary of my career—
>>I give thanks.

There are so many bonuses besides the paycheck.
>New interests bring new insights, and I find myself
>growing in spite of myself.

>It's easier for me to see the kids growing up, know-
>ing that even when the nest is empty, I will have
>meaningful work of my own to do. Even now I
>have tales of my own to swap about "what hap-
>pened at school today."

>My days are full, busy, and happy, and more varied
>than ever before.

Dear Lord, you know it isn't all roses. Lots of things
I need to do go undone. But some of them weren't
very important anyway. And, oh, the unexpected
bonuses of this double life I lead!

I didn't have to get a job to be "fulfilled," but I did
have to get a job.
>Thank you for the fulfillment that is one of the
>bonuses.

Amen.

Lord,

    I need to enlarge the place of my tent, and stretch out the curtains of my habitation . . .

        for I have confined my love, my concern, within the four walls of my own household . . .
        I minister sincerely to the needs of my family; but I manage to remain undisturbed by the needs of all others . . .
        I lavish love and care on these who are "mine"—forgetting conveniently that those outside are also mine.

Dear Lord, help me enlarge the place of my tent. Help me reach beyond my own front door to include those whom I have shut out of my concern.

        They're there, Lord, needing to be *included*. But my mind has been closed. I haven't really cared that they were there,

            thirsty or unemployed—
            lonely or unloved.

        Haunt me with their need. Burden me with their loneliness

            until I *dare* take responsibility for them,
            until I enlarge the place of my tents.

                          Amen.

It comes as a clear admonition, Lord . . .
    "Judge not."
But I do judge,
    try by self-appointed jury of self,
        and condemn—
            all in an instant.
And why, Lord?
What is this bias that causes me to classify people?
    and pigeonhole people?
        and then accept without challenge the automatic
        condemnation that my prejudice metes out?
What is this self-conceit that makes me consider my-
    self *wise* enough to judge?
        or *good* enough to judge?
Why do I assume that the fellow who thinks in dif-
    ferent symbols, thinks "funny"?
Why do I insist that the kid who marches to a dif-
    ferent drummer is out of step?
Must all yardsticks be the same as mine?
    All symbols?
        All interpretations of symbols?
            All rhythms?
                All the same as mine?
I know the admonition, Lord.
But I forget.
I shift my mind to automatic, and it goes right on
    making oversimplified generalizations and pre-
    computed judgments . . . which I accept without
    question.

                Ah, Lord—
                            forgive.

God,

> there are some people who give, expecting a return
> on their giving—either of brownie points or of a
> like gift.

But there are others who truly *give*—

> who out of a basic trust in the universe, open their
> hearts, their pocketbooks, and their pantries
>> and offer whatever they have to whoever
>> needs it.

Lord, they've blessed my life . . .

> with good, hot homemade bread;
> with anonymous financial help when the wolf
> howled at our door;
> and with the wondrous gift of the listening ear and
> understanding heart.

And it's not just *me* who receives of their bounty—

> it's everyone—
> it's anyone who needs their love and care.

They are never too busy.

They seem to have an abundance of strength.

And even their sometimes meager supply of loaves
and fishes seems inexhaustible.

Their cup runneth over with a goodness that returns
to bless them, too—

> a return neither asked for nor expected.
> And they wonder that they should have been so
> blessed.

Oh, I thank you for those who give!

Amen, amen!

You already know, dear Father, how much he means to me—this dear husband of mine.

You know how he has helped me far beyond anything required by law or tradition. He never felt changing diapers or washing dishes was beneath him, if the job needed to be done. And I thank you for the conversations we've had at the baby's crib or the kitchen sink.

He's always been out ahead of me in "things of the spirit" but has never made me feel like a laggard.

And he's shared insights with me, and choice knowledge that I had not been able to gain for myself.

He's not "too tired" to go for bike rides with the kids—

    not too busy to remember thoughtful offerings of love—

    often—

      an ice cream cone,

      a couple of daisies.

He's the one whose eyes shine with pride in me when I have a small success—

    and whose strong arms support me when failure flattens my ego.

He's the steady rock, the sparkle of fun, the enabler —friend, lover, cohort.

I don't *really* believe marriages are made in heaven,

Lord, but surely he has been for me what I have needed. I doubt that it was "remarkable insight" on my part. Perhaps it was sheer happenstance.

However our marriage happened, Father, I thank you over and over for this wonderful husband of mine.

                Amen.

Ah, Lord—is this, then, the Christian message?
  that I can *celebrate life*—
  with any other living soul—
  just because he is, as I am, a living soul, and a
    child of thine?
Ah, so!
  I can *celebrate* life—for it is good.
  I can marvel that you should have created us so—
    free to goof—
    free to *live* creatively—
    free to respond to thee—
        celebrating our sonship with the dance of
        life.
Lord,
  I affirm the goodness of life.
  And I affirm the goodness of mankind.
  For all that is past, I give thanks—for it has
    brought me to this moment.
  For all that lies ahead, I say *Yes!*—for *thy* word
    is that life is something to rejoice about and
    that the rejoicing can be shared—must be
    shared!

                    Thank you, Lord.
                    Alleluia!

Lord, God, I am disquieted within me.
> There is much in my world that is unsettled and
> unsettling, and I find myself going about with a
> cloud of vaguely defined troubles just over my
> head.
>> But it shuts out the sun!
I brood over the cloud,
> and travel in valleys of shadow—
unaware that the sun still shines,
> and forgetting in my preoccupation that thou art
> with me.

Ah, so. I shall call my cloud of troubles to account.
What *are* the things that disquiet me, Lord?
Confronting them reveals some as impostors—
> groundless worries that can be dispelled.
Confronting them reveals others as beyond my scope
> —things I can do nothing about. Those, too, I can
> dismiss.
All that remains are my own legitimate cares.
> These I can face, Lord, now that I see them more
> clearly.
> These I can attend to, or begin to work on—
>> for they are no longer a cloud of vague and
>> nameless worries.
>>> They are specific tasks.
>>> And on them, and on me, shines the now-
>>> permitted sun.
Thank you, God, for this new day.

> > > > Amen.

Dear Lord, perhaps it's the doing it *consciously* that makes the difference.

She calls it Holy Thursday.

Sometimes she visits a convalescent home—
or spends the afternoon in the children's ward at city hospital—
sometimes she just sits in the park and soaks up the sunshine.

But she does it consciously, Lord—
deliberately undertaking a portion of the day as an act of worship.

For she has to work on Sunday,
and Thursday is her sabbath.

And I . . . who do not have to go to work on Sundays . . . allow myself to slip unconsciously into a routine pattern, and sometimes not actually participate in worship at all.

Holy Thursday?
Holy Sunday?
Lord, help me undertake a portion of *my* sabbath *consciously,* as an act of worship.

Amen.

Dear Lord,
>I give thanks for this little child—
>>for her wide-eyed inquiry—
>>for the openness with which she accepts others—
>>for the artless honesty with which she lives out her days.

Her path has crossed mine only for this short while, but knowing her has been one of those unexpected bonuses that life has to offer.

Ah, Lord, I have much to learn from her.
>She chuckles often—for no other reason than her awareness that her world is good—
>>that she is loved.
>She loves others, as naturally as flowers open to sun.
>>There is no discrimination to her love—
>>no embarrassment in expressing it.
>And she's curious, Lord—
>>alive—
>>awake to what is around her,
>>and to the delightful possibilities of it all.

Ah, Lord—
>I give thanks for this little child.

Amen.

Lord, why is it that I try so doggedly to deceive *myself?*

    I magnify my accomplishments and overlook my faults;

    I refuse to acknowledge my possibilities,
        refuse to accept the gifts that are mine.

    I work hard at building a self-image—
        and foist it off *even on me.*

Except that I am not totally successful.

    Oh, Lord, you know that I am not *really* deceived.

    A gullible part of me honors the image I've tried to create.

    But my other, deeper consciousness is aware of the deception.

        And I am twain.

        Fragmented.

        And therefore frustrated.

Is it that I cannot bear to see me as I really am?

    If you can accept me—knowing me—why is it that I cannot accept myself? Perhaps I have not ever really tried.

        It would be much simpler than living this double life—than trying to keep up the complicated subterfuge.

                        Help me.
                        Amen.

Unwittingly we do these things, Lord.
Unconsciously we tread upon another's day.
My child, my friend—even a new acquaintance—
   approaches with an experience to share—
      an offering of self—
   and I belittle it by not listening.
   Or I depreciate it by topping it with a bigger story
    of my own.
   Unwittingly.
Lord, I don't *intend* to squelch, or belittle others,
   or to tread heavily—ever—
   upon their tender moments.
But I do it—
and I see the bewilderment, the hurt,
   that I have caused.
And there is no way I can undo it—
   no way I can unsay what I have said.
    Father, forgive.
It isn't altogether *unwittingly*.
   Part of me is still feeding my own ego
    at the expense of others.
   Part of me—submerged but not suppressed—
    continues to sacrifice the feelings, even of those
    dear to me, to the petty god of self.

Father, forgive my "unwitting" cruelties.

                  Amen.

Lord,

I'd have thought that a college girl wouldn't have
time to squander on an eleven-year-old—
    nor the perception to *see* her carefully controlled
    homesickness.

But Peggy did. She offered her listening ear—
    and stayed for a long time of quiet conversation—
    something, I suppose, a camp counselor *should* do.

But after camp was over, she reached out again—
    and the letter she wrote was warm, and newsy—
        "just between us friends."

        My child feels more worthy now, than she has
        ever felt before—
            and more grown-up—
    and it's quite likely that she will never need to be
    homesick again, for she has discovered that in
    her world are people who care.

Thank you, God, for the Peggys in this world—who
reach out naturally to others, and who respond as
naturally to the real needs of those around them.
Thank you for people who *accept* people, without
condescension or "tolerance"—but who see them as
they are, as persons of worth.

    In doing so they have a way of adding blessed-
    ness to the lives of the rest of us.

                        Thank you, Lord.
                        Amen.

Dear Lord,
  I bit off more than I can chew—
    and now I've got to chew it.
  I have undertaken more than one person should—
    but it needs doing, Lord—
    and I am here.
  So . . . I come asking strength.

Lord, I shall need the cobwebs cleared from my mind.
I shall need to be able to separate the essentials from the nonessentials, so that I can zero in on the things that must be done.
I shall need a sense of humor, to keep my perspective, and to keep me from taking myself or my task *too* seriously.
And I shall need strength, Lord—to do the task that I have undertaken to do in thy name.
These things I ask.

Amen.

I thank you, God,
>   for the impossible dream—
>   for the unreachable sky.

Sometimes I get frustrated because I haven't "arrived,"
>   because I cannot ever quite *achieve* my goals.

But I am grateful, Lord, that the dream *is* impossible,
>   and that the sky *is* beyond my earth-bound reach.

I am grateful, Lord, that *you* are beyond my comprehending.
>   If I could understand you, with my so-mortal mind, then you would be only a god—and not . . . God!
>   You *are* always the Mystery . . .
>>   always beyond me . . .
>>   always eluding me . . .
>>>   but always luring me on to new awareness, new comprehension.
>   You leave me unsatisfied,
>>   but you lead me on.
>   You give a center to my being, which, alone, makes life coherent.
>   You undergird me with a love which will not let me go, and from which I do not wish to escape.

Understandable gods and reachable dreams
>   lose their significance.

But thou art Mystery!
>   Oh, Lord, my God, I give thee thanks.

>>>>>   Amen.

Ah, Lord—
   a blessed time to be alone.

I forget, in the bustle and hustle of busy days, that I
   need it—that it is as necessary to my emotional
   equilibrium as food is to my body. I hunger for it.
      And when I deny myself this aloneness—which
      I do in the name of getting-on-with-the-task—
      I become jumpy and irritable, unable to *perform*
      the task.

Ah, Lord—
   a blessed time to be alone.
First, it's just a time to unwind,
   and then, somehow, it becomes prelude to prayer.
It becomes a time to center down, to re-orient my day.
I thank you, God, for the blessed renewal of my times
   alone.

And help me remember that everyone within this
   household needs aloneness. Let me remember to
   not intrude—to hush a minute—
   and to provide the possibility of times alone—
   for my husband,
      for my children,
         for me.

                                          Amen.

Dear Lord,

    I, too, am compelled to lament, I don't know how
    to love you.

    I just don't know how.

The patriarchs insisted that I must love you with my
whole *heart*.

        But *my* heart isn't whole. It's divided up into
        neat sections . . .

            and you know, before I confess it, that one
            of the larger ones is labeled *"self."*

    Lord, how *can* I love thee?

    How *can* I harness my wayward will?

"And with all my *soul*," the patriarchs insisted.

    This I understand even less.

    "Soul" and "heart" both seem to be symbols for
    that indefinable part of me over which I have
    so little control.

The next part I *understand* clearly enough; I just
can't do it.

    "With all my *strength?*" Ah, Lord—what shall I
    eat, then, or with what shall I feed my children?
    And wherewithal shall we be clothed? With *all*
    my strength?

        Oh, the stipulations are hard indeed.

And then thy Son added another . . . that I
    should love thee with all my *mind* . . .

        that I should put all the scientific training and
        academic schooling and *every mental power*
        I've got into my love for thee.

            Ah, so. You do not ask me to deny the
            mind you have given me; you only ask that
            I *use it all* to love.

And how can I do all that . . . when I've got to
remember to pay the bills? My daily lists are long
ones, and my mind is stayed on them . . .
and not on thee.
And yet, Lord . . . thou knowest that I love thee.
Help me express my love *through* the daily-ness
of my life, and not in spite of it.
Accept the mundane tasks that are mine to do,
as an expression of my love for thee.

Amen.

I guess I've always been aware, Lord, that hope alone isn't enough. For there is no virtue in my sitting back and wishing for—or even *expecting*— a better world tomorrow . . . if that is all I do.
And yet . . . I *do* sit, and hope—and expect you to "make everything all right."

Hope is all very good—but it won't move mountains. And there are mountains to be moved if our hopes are going to happen.
Mountains to be moved?
Hmm. I seem to remember something about *faith* moving mountains. And no namby-pamby faith at that—but a hard-nosed, sleeves-rolled-up, clear-eyed faith . . . that *sees* all the problems, but believes that there are solutions, too . . . and pursues those solutions steadfastly.

Ah, so, Lord. Help me put *that* kind of faith into action, to back up the things for which I hope.

Amen.

Father,

Grant a special blessing on those who teach our children this year.

Theirs is not an easy task, and it doesn't reap much day-to-day glory.

But the influence they have on my children is second only to my own.

Sometimes they can utter a word, and it becomes gospel.

Sometimes they can breathe life into an author or an issue or a set of problems or instill an idea that becomes a determining factor for a whole life-style.

May they be aware of—and use carefully—the power that is concentrated in them.

And may I remember to *express* my appreciation, my thanks, my gratitude to them. How rarely have I done so—and yet how very much I owe to those men and women who have encouraged, disciplined, and challenged our children,

and who have enticed them to learn.

Amen.

Father—
    It becomes very clear to me now that I had not
    really accepted him as a *person*.
        His sour attitude had been a source of irrita-
        tion to me for all these years—and I'd just
        called him "that man in the hardware store."
            And dismissed him.
But today we talked—and he *became* a person.
    I learned that he helped build the highway north
    of town, forty years ago—pulled a "Fresno" with
    a team of mules.
        And all this time I hadn't even realized he
        had a name.

Ah, Lord—I go about so blindly . . .
    not recognizing the *humanity* in those around
      me—
    the spirit of adventure—
    the drama—
      that is part of their lives.
    And I dismiss them—
    and am thereby impoverished.
        Forgive.

                        Amen.

I think she's waiting, Lord,
   for a "call" from thee—
   an engraved invitation,
   clearly explicating what you'd have her do.
And I remember waiting, so—confident that I could
   do *anything under heaven,* if I were just *sure*
   that's what you wanted.
And I remember waiting . . .
   frustrated at not *knowing* . . .
   and, in a way, relieved of responsibility, because
      of not *knowing.*
And I remember waiting.

I thank you, Lord, for whoever it was, those quite-a-
   few-years-ago, who spoke of two lines intersect-
   ing. The long one, he said, was the needs of the
   world; the other was my own ability.
      And where they intersected, *there was my call.*
Ah, so. There *is* my call.
When I look at it in this light, it comes with un-
   avoidable clarity.
      Why else would you have given me ability?
      Why else would you have given me the sighted-
         ness, that I should even be aware of the
         needs?
Not all of us *get* engraved invitations,
   but somewhere "talent" and "need" intersect.
There is thy call.
   For me.
   For her.
   For all of us.

                              Amen.

Father,
It is good to *belong* to a family,
   good to be linked to the family of my past,
      undergirded by their tradition,
      backed by their wisdom,
      supported by their confidence in me.

It is *good* to *have* a family,
   good to be linked to the future by my children
      who walk boldly into a world I know only
      through them. They create new traditions that
      will be meaningful for us all—
         and they both look to me for guidance and
         share with me the new wisdom they gain.
And I am, again, supported by their confidence.

And it is good to *create* a family,
   to link myself by an act of volition to those of my
      present—
         adopting some *not* kin to me, because of a
            spark—or a need—that unites us,
         or *accepting* the offer of adoption from the
            lonely old couple down the street. Or the
            in-and-out, omnipresent child-friend, who
            can unwind at our house.
I thank you, Lord, that it will never be necessary
   for me to be totally alone—
      for I am linked to the past,
         to the future,
            and to the present
               by *family* ties.

                              Amen.

Bleaugh!
Not much of a way to begin a prayer, Lord . . .
    but the raucous BLRRRNG of that alarm clock
    is not much of a way to begin a day, either.
        I notice that it does not rouse the poet in me,
        to greet the new dawn;
            it summons instead the rebel in me.
            I get up belligerently, jaw set, teeth
            clenched, fists doubled.
And it's the same new battle every morning.
And yet . . .
    I hate, later on, to have *not* got up! Sleeping *too*
    much just makes me disgruntled—heavy-
    headed and slow to recover.

Hmm.
Thinking it over *now,* while it isn't ringing, I am
    aware that the alarm isn't really fiendish; it's just
    efficient—doing what I asked it to do.
        The problem's not the clock, Lord—it's me . . .
        it's my reluctance to pay the small price of
        shaking myself awake . . .
            in exchange for this new day!
Ah, Lord, rouse in me that sense of adventure that
    makes me greet exuberantly *each* unrepeatable
    day!

                    Amen.

Dear Lord,
    Lest I be too easily miffed,
    help me remember that the fleas come with the
    dog.

Some days I get hung up on the fleas.
    I bluster and stew about the petty irritations that
    are an *inherent part* of the things I really want.
        And that's rather senseless.

So help me, Lord.
    Help me sit still long enough, in thy presence, to
    be perfectly clear about what I want to do.
        And then I won't find the fleas so irritating.
If my home is to be a haven for my family,
    then I must accept a few of the inconveniences
    involved in keeping it a pleasant place.
        But if it *is* a *haven,* then the "inconveniences"
        are well worth the effort they require.
If what I want is a long life, with time to *do* all the
    things I've been saving until I had time to do
    them, then help me accept with grace the "incon-
    veniences" of growing older.

I guess it's a matter of putting the fleas into perspec-
    tive, Lord.
    Help me remember how little they are.

Amen.

Dear Lord,

The radio prophet said that we have only seventeen months until the Second Coming.

Well . . . I'm not convinced, for "no man knoweth the hour or the day . . ."

But if it *were* true, Lord, *how would you want me to spend my seventeen months?*

> Tidying up my affairs?
> Praying for my own salvation?
> Or getting on with the work you'd have me do?

St. Francis said he'd keep on hoeing the garden.

If I, like St. Francis, have decided what the task is, then the "seventeen months" need not alarm me, for I shall simply keep on working.

And I would pray that the work itself would be a witness to thee. This, after all, is what the *valid* task must be.

> The hoeing of the garden, the doing of the task, should be done *in thy name.*
>
> I need not wear a *sign,* or carry a poster.
>
> And I do not wish to badger people with my much speaking.
>
> But there may be occasion, Lord, when I have the opportunity to say, quite simply, that what I do, I do for the Living Lord . . .
>> until the end of my days
>> whether that be seventeen months,
>> or more,
>> or less.

Amen.

Dear Lord,

    I have been chastised—

    and by a little old lady who had the audacity to turn off her hearing aid in the midst of my argument.

    I have never been more frustrated!

But the chastisement comes only now, after I've had time to mull it over. I *deserved* being turned off.

    I was done-by-as-I-do.

And I do it to those I love best.

    I have only now become aware of how often I *turn off* my children.

        One comes to tell me an involved incident that happened at school—and my face listens while my mind goes right on planning the supper menus.

            Or I hear suddenly, with my mostly turned-off ears, the real concern in "What do *you* think, Mom?"

Ah, Lord—how terribly frustrating it must be to them that I tune them out.

    I deny them when I do so.

    I dehumanize them.

    And I must frustrate them, as I was frustrated by the turned-off hearing aid.

I give most people at least a *little* closer attention than I do these whom it is my happy *duty* to guide and counsel.

    Ah—Father—I have turned deaf ears to my own children.

Forgive.

Ah, Lord—

Brother Lawrence said he *"practiced* the presence of God."

Then, yes.

Now? I'm not so sure.

Could he do so even in the dentist's chair?

Even in the five o'clock traffic?

Life is considerably more complicated today.

You know, Lord, this is my excuse.

And yet—Brother Lawrence *practiced* the art of keeping his mind stayed on thee.

And I could, too.

Even in the dentist's chair. What better place! Often the dentist himself walks out and leaves me alone and it is quiet, and peaceful, with none of the I-ought-to-be-up-doing-the-dishes distractions of home. And I *could* use that moment of stillness to center down on thy love. But I don't. I never think of it.

And then, when the dentist comes back, I *still* could practice thy presence, Lord. I certainly can't *talk,* with my mouth full of fingers and tools . . . but I could "think on thee"—and intentionally, at that moment, give thanks for a number of things—including dentists.

Practice thy presence?

Even in the five o'clock traffic? That's certainly no time of peace and quiet. And yet—you are there, too, Lord. And I can focus my grasshopper mind *in-thy-name* on those around me.

They are thy people—beside whom I drive.

Some of them are in a hurry, too. They have
worries, problems—like mine—more so?
Ah, Lord, bless them—
and bless me
with thy presence.

Amen.

So I said "yes," Lord,
"Yes, I'll teach the class."
   And now I'm getting cold feet.
   And fluttery insides.
   And I wish to goodness I'd said no!
Well . . . only in weaker moments. I'm glad, really,
that I said yes. I hadn't intended to. Until, some-
how, I was struck with a feeling of oughtness.
   And I said yes.
   And I'm glad I did.
   Only now I need help.
      Still the fluttering of my insides, Lord.
      Sharpen my mind that I may play the part
         of the whetstone,
      and sharpen in turn the minds of these Sun-
         day scholars, on behalf of whom I have
         said yes.
I ask thy guidance, Lord.
Ah, so. Now I shall go do my homework.

                             Amen.

Lord,
how is it that *my* child can irritate me to the point of distraction, doing the very same thing that I would find tolerable—even understandable—in my neighbor's child?

Is the act more aggravating with my child than with another? Or just that I am more uptight about it?

Ah, Lord, I have prayed—and I pray still—for self-unity.

And yet, in this regard, I need to be twins—
with one of me here nearby to love and challenge and *enjoy* my children,
and the other one of me over yonder somewhere, able to guide and discipline from a distance.

Father, God, grant me the objectivity that I *must* have, if I am to be fair with my child.

Help me see him from a little distance.

And help me see him as a person in his own right, not as an extension of myself.

I can love and enjoy my child from right here, Lord—but help me achieve the distance I need for his discipline.

Amen.

God,
those are *persons*—not robots—in cars traveling by mine.

The *cars* are machines, but they are driven by live, warm-blooded human beings—
who also have errands to run,
and schedules to meet—
who also have worries that rest heavily upon their minds.

Let me not forget.
I do. I forget they are people.

I look upon them as *machines,*
a number of which are in my way—
as *machines,*
not deserving of a second thought.

What is it that is so dehumanizing about buckling myself to a car? I become part of it—
turn in my humanity for awhile—put myself into gear and drive like an automaton.

Lord, *I am not a machine.* And neither are those other people.

Forgive my inhuman disregard.

And help me establish the pattern of putting the key in the ignition in an attitude of prayer, of reminding myself of the humanity I share with those others who will also be driving this day.

Keep me clearheaded enough to drive responsibly, and *human* enough to drive compassionately.

Every time.

Amen.

Dear Lord,

I do not recall a single beatitude about "blessed are the gluttonous"—

and yet I pursue my favorite indoor-outdoor sport with enthusiasm. *Eating* is a necessity for life, and (I have a hunch) divinely intended to be a *pleasant* necessity;

but I have allowed it to become a besetting sin. I pile my plate with calorically forbidding delectables—and then later on, look with dismay at the rising numbers on the bathroom scale.

And I yearn for chocolate pie in a way that I never seem to yearn for worthier prizes.

Blessed are the *dieters,* Lord?

Perhaps that's the way it would read.

Blessed are those who deny themselves the fleeting taste of a candy bar in order that they might be in shape for the task.

Blessed are the dieters,

who manage to keep things in perspective.

And count me in.

Amen.

Father,
There are times when someone else can be for my child what he needs—

> when his friend's dad—or some other adult—can discuss with him in a new way those things about which he already knows *my* opinion.

> > And each *listens* to the other, with new ears.
> > The encounter is person-to-person, rather than parent-to-child.

And *good* comes of it—and a new understanding.

I give thanks, Lord, for those who have done this for my child;

> who have seen beyond his belly-achin'—
> > or his passivity—
> > > a worth he himself could not recognize,
> and who have given him a new self-image,
> helped him take a new step toward maturity.

> > Theirs is a ministry of presence, Lord.
> > They have simply *been* there, when he needed them.

I give thanks for them, Lord,
> and for their ministering.

Amen.

"It's difficult to be entertaining," the speaker said,
  "two days in a row."
And I laughed, because I know how he feels.
And then I wondered, why do I feel I *have* to be
  entertaining, anyway?

Ah, Lord, I try so hard to keep up the act.
I'd like to be thought of as scintillating—
    delightful—
      such *fun* to be with.
And I try—ad exhaustion!
    But that's not really the sort of person I am.

Hmm . . .
    Maybe I haven't really *discovered* the sort of per-
    son I am,
        for I'd also like to be one of those serene
        persons, so that when I come into a room,
        people are calmed by my very presence.
    You know, Lord, I'm not really *that* either.

Not really scintillating, not quite serene.
    Somewhere, in between, is me.

And what I *ought* to want is to be whatever it is I
really am.
Ah, Lord, there is a certain clarity that comes with
  the admission of my play-acting.
It's quite likely that if I quit thinking about what *I*
  am—and put my concern on other people,
  then I might *know* who I am.
And besides, I would be relieved of the burden of
  having to be "entertaining,
    two days in a row."

                                        Amen.

Lord,
  she carried a cross in the pocket of her purse.
I guess she had done so for years,
  but I don't think any of us were aware of it.

It wasn't a talisman,
  and it wasn't a good luck charm.
    It was just a reminder of who she was,
    and what she was about.

I've really never wanted to carry a cross . . . like
that . . .
I don't *need* a talisman,
  or a good luck charm.
That kind of "magic" simply isn't for real.
  But, Lord, I *do* need a reminder, even as she did.
  I forget who I am,
    and what I'm about.
    My attention wanders—sometimes for days.
  I get sidetracked—go off in hot pursuit on point-
    less little tangents of my own—
      until, later—
        sometimes *much* later—
      I become aware of how stale life has become—
      and I am *reminded* who I am,
        and whose I am.
Whether or not I carry a cross, or a cryptic fish, or a
mustard seed, or any other symbol of thy love in
my pocket—
    let me not forget . . .
      thy love . . .

                                        Amen.

Lord,
 it must have been a dozen years ago that I said
 it—
  but she remembers.
I had forgotten all about it,
 until her letter came, thanking me for a single
 sentence—
  a single sentence spoken during a bus ride,
  years ago—
   but she remembers.
It shook me up—
 that she still carries that sentence around in her
 mind.
It calls me to accountability for my words—
 so many of which are hastily, thoughtlessly
 spoken.
Lord, God, let me be mindful of what I say—
 even in casual conversation—
 even in jest—
  that I do not unthinkingly hurt
  or wound
  or wrongly influence
   one who might hear—
   and remember.

Amen.

Lord,
  I've spent a good deal of my life waiting
    till things got better—
    till I finished school—
    till the kids got past "this stage"—
    till we got the promotion—
  sure that *then* I would really be able to enjoy life.
How unperceptive of me!
  This is life.
  This is the only moment I have, right now.
    Let me enjoy it—
      savor it—
        consciously.
  If it gets away—unsavored—
    it's gone forever.
    And life becomes a dull, wearisome parade of
      unrelished days.
But I forget.
I Bissell the bedroom rug when I might be dancing
  to the music of the spheres!
I empty the garbage without even seeing the sky,
  or feeling the earth,
  without sensing the smell of approaching rain,
  without hearing the locust's cheery song
    . . . and emptying the garbage becomes a real
    drag.

Ah, Lord,
  this is my moment!
  All I shall ever know of life is made up of *such
  little moments* as this.
    Let me seize and savor every one.

                                        Amen.

Dear Lord,

Deliver me from the cult of the tranquilized—and let me not use *prayer* as a sedative.

It almost sounds like the thing to do—

> for I have been taught to come to you with all my problems—and surely up-tightness is one of them.

But to "take" prayer, as I would an aspirin, at bed-time, strikes me suddenly as an abuse of a holy privilege.

Ah, Lord—it is so *right* that I come to thee in prayer.

> It is so *right* that I bring my tensions as well as my joy and thanksgiving to thee.

There are times when I have gone as far as I can, and my real *need* is to unwind, in thy presence— to get myself and my problems into perspective.

But if I come asking thee to "make it all go away, so I can sleep tonight"—

> if I *use* prayer solely as a tranquilizer,
>
> I have missed the boat.

Thy call is not to tranquility,

> but to a hazardous task,
>
> undertaken *with thee!*

I would not miss the thrill of participation in such a venture of the spirit!

> It is not sedation I need,
>
> > but a daily new awareness of thy presence!
> >
> > So be it.

Amen.

Lord,
I *do* let my heart be troubled!
And I *do* permit it to be disquieted within me.
  For the times are out of joint—
  and unruffled composure seems singularly inappropriate.

Lord, I think you did not call us to quiescence at times like these.
You gave us eyes to see—
  and minds to comprehend—
    and hearts to move us to do the necessary deed.

So? My disquieted heart is a gift?
  I am *divinely* disturbed?
I thank you, Lord, that my heart still *can* be troubled.
  Only so can I be sensitive to the aching needs around me.

Then let me not misunderstand my troubled heart,
  not permit uneasy fears to paralyze my motor centers,
  or to distort my judgments.
Let me rather do everything I can—
  everything I possibly can—
    to accomplish the necessary deed . . . and then leave it in thy hands.

                                    Amen.

My times are in thy hands,
oh, Lord, I wish them there.

I thank you, God,
for the roundness of things—
for the way that day gentles into night—
for the transition of Indian summer.
I think I could not adjust to a square world,
where the turning of a sudden corner would
thrust me into winter.
I thank you that growing up was like this, too—
no sudden corners between my childtime and
youth,
between youth and adulthood.
How traumatic *those* square corners would have
been!

I am grateful, Lord.
I am grateful for the transitions.
There is a certain rightness about the dawn that
eases me into day—
and the in-between ages that enable me to make my
own preparation for the seasons that lie ahead.

I give thanks for the roundness of life.

Amen.

Father,
   Now I lay me down to sleep—
   gratefully—
   relishing the gentle flexing of tired muscles,
   relishing the feel of cool sheets—
   grateful for night.

I relinquish now the control I have exercised all day
   over my mind.
I let it wander as it will,
   not knowing *where* it will wander,
   nor on what it will dwell,
   nor with what problems it will continue to grapple.

I commit my subconscious mind into thy keeping—
   for thine are the days—
   and thine also the night—
      and I am thine.

Now I lay me down to sleep.

                                        Amen.

Father,
>   She asked me who he was, and I didn't know.
>   We talked instead of other things. But *even as we
>   talked,* the amazing computer that is my mind be-
>   gan flipping through the files of faces in its
>   memory bank . . . and quite suddenly—without
>   conscious summons—it produced the answer. Oh,
>   he's the fellow we met one night at the Smiths,
>   three . . . or was it four . . . years ago.

Ah, Lord!

I am awed by the astonishing possibilities of this
computer I carry around inside my head.

It registers experiences of which I am only dimly
aware—processes data I haven't even noticed—
records it all—
>   files it systematically, somehow,
>>   this kaleidoscopic record of everything I have
>>   ever read, done, thought, felt, heard, seen,
>>   or wondered about.
>   And then it flips through all that,
>>   and dredges up the right recollection . . .
>>>   without my even being aware that the com-
>>>   puter is turned on.

I am awed—and astonished—and fascinated—and
humbled.

>   How you must have loved us!
>   How much you must have expected of us!
>   How much more-than-animals you must have ex-
>   pected us to be—
>   how much more-than-mechanical-devices you
>   must have expected us to be,
>>   to have entrusted to each of us such a

computer-with-feeling,
computer-with-love.
    I am awed,
        astonished,
        grateful,
        challenged.

Amen.

Lord,
I'm so far behind with little things that have to be
   done that I'm close to tears.

Little things!
Stupid little things.

   Like catsup on the kitchen floor.
   And the three dozen things piled up on my
      dresser to be put away.
   I can't remember to buy a new little glass knob for
      the coffeepot, and I have to plug the hole with
      a piece of sheet—
         which becomes a hot, soggy, dribbly mess.

Oh, Lord, deliver me!
What can I *do* about this tyranny of trivia?
   Blubber over it?
   Panic?
   Throw up my hands in despair?
   Be driven to tears?
      Or can I, perhaps, face it with composure—
      and maybe even turn the tyranny into a picnic?

Let's see—
   if I gathered up the kids, and we made a TRIP to
   the coffeepot-lid-store,
         we could drop off the cluttery Coke bottles
         on the way there,
            and stop at the library on the way back.

   Mayhap we could *sing* en route,
      and laugh (at the trivia? at the tyranny? at the

fun of just being alive?)
and still get back in time to attend to the
splotch of catsup on the kitchen floor.

Ah, Lord, I thank you for this day!

Amen.

Ah, Lord,

I'd forgotten, somehow—since last year—how *many* blossoms there can be on a crab apple tree.

I'd forgotten how *many* ruffly-edged disks of new-green seeds a single elm bestows.

It's this largess, this unstinting generosity, that boggles the mind. I'm awed anew, every spring, for it always comes as a wonder, and I'm never quite prepared for the bounty of it.

It would seem that in a world so lavish with its gifts I would be less begrudging with my own.

There's a freshness, and a zest, and an open-to-lifeness about spring that I would emulate.

Amen.